TH RAWN

For my father, Lloyd Andrew Gibbs (1911–1989),
and Jay-Jay, one of the much-loved Holsteins
on our Minnesota dairy farm
—P.A.

For Karen
—S.J. & L.F.

Text copyright © 2012 by Phyllis E. Alsdurf
Jacket art and interior illustrations copyright © 2012 by Steve Johnson and Lou Fancher

All rights reserved. Published in the United States by Random House Children's Books, a division of Random House, Inc., New York.

Random House and the colophon are registered trademarks of Random House, Inc.

Visit us on the Web! www.randomhouse.com/kids

Educators and librarians, for a variety of teaching tools, visit us at www.randomhouse.com/teachers

Library of Congress Cataloging-in-Publication Data
Alsdurf, Phyllis, 1950–.
It's milking time / by Phyllis Alsdurf ; illustrations by Steve Johnson and Lou Fancher. — 1st ed.
p. cm.
Summary: A young girl spends a day helping her father milk their cows, as she does throughout the year.
ISBN 978-0-375-86911-2 (trade) — ISBN 978-0-375-96911-9 (lib. bdg.) — ISBN 978-0-375-89993-5 (ebook)
[1. Farm life—Fiction. 2. Cows—Fiction. 3. Milking—Fiction. 4. Fathers and daughters—Fiction.]
I. Johnson, Steve, 1960– ill. II. Fancher, Lou, ill. III. Title.
PZ7.A46263Its 2012 [E]—dc22 2010047772

MANUFACTURED IN CHINA

10 9 8 7 6 5 4 3 2 1

First Edition

It's Milking Time

By Phyllis Alsdurf

Illustrations by Steve Johnson & Lou Fancher

RANDOM HOUSE NEW YORK

*Every morning, every night,
it's milking time.*

I slip under barbed wire
and race down the lane.
Fast.
I'm late.
Dad's waiting on me
to start milking.
"Come, boss," I holler.
"Come, boss."
There by a stand of poplars,
a huddle of black and white
starts to move.
Jay-Jay, as usual,
leads the Holstein parade.

Single file they come,
on the same worn path.
"Come, boss, come, boss.
It's milking time."

Cuds a-chewing,

tails a-swatting,

hooves a-pounding,

into the barnyard they trudge.

I close the gate
and head to the barn,
where Dad piles grain
in front of each stall.
I scoop soybean meal on top
and set up the milkers.
Together we lay down a bed
of fresh straw.
Outside, the cows
bellow and snort.
"Ready," Dad says,
and I open the barn door.

Impatient and hungry,
the cows heave themselves into the barn.
Their hooves clack
across the cement floor.
We swat rumps to keep them moving,
to the same places every time.
I lock each cow in her stanchion.
Dad washes off teats.

A is for Alphie, always first
to be hooked up to a milker.
A leather strap across her back
holds it in place.

Every morning, every night,
it's milking time.

I lean against a dusty windowsill

and see sunlight setting

on a field of corn.

Dad's arm rests on my shoulders.

"Sure could use some rain," he says.

The air is hot, heavy.

Overhead a fan whirs.

Tails swishing,

the cows chomp and chew their cud.

Dad turns on the radio, low,

so we can hear the weather report,

or maybe

the ball game.

I hear the slurp of suction—Alphie's done.
"Time for Bertha," I yell to Dad.
Alphie, Bertha, Cassie, Di . . .
an alphabet of cows to milk.
Each time a milker fills,
Dad empties it into a pail that he carries,
arm outstretched for balance,
to the milk house.

A cascade of blue and white
empties into the strainer
and gurgles through
to the milk can below.
Dad pours some into a pitcher
to take up to the house
when milking time is done.
Underfoot, cats lap up foamy spills.

Every morning, every night,
it's milking time.

In a corner pen,
a half dozen calves
wobble awkwardly
on legs spindly and weak.
They bawl for attention,
and shove their boxy heads
between worn wooden slats
as they nuzzle for food.

Feeding them is my job—
something Dad lets me do
all by
myself.

I fill their trough with a pyramid of grain

and unravel a bale of hay.

Dad hands me a pail,

heavy with milk for the calves.

I climb into the pen,

and a small calf

with a triangle of white above his nose

bumps against me.

"Looks like you've got yourself a friend," Dad laughs

as he moves a milker to the next cow.

The calf gives a baby moo.

"What do you want to name the little guy?"

The calf nudges my leg,
and I wrap my arm around his neck.
He looks up at me with liquid brown eyes.
"Buddy," I say.

Every morning, every night,
it's milking time.

Soon every cow's been milked,

and two,

three,

four cans have been filled.

One by one we unhook stanchions.

"Go on, girls. Get outta here," says Dad.

"Tch, tch," I urge from behind.

"Move on out to pasture."

Then the barn is empty.

A swallow swoops

through an open window

and out again.

We shovel manure into gutters
so the paddles of the barn cleaner
can carry it to a waiting spreader.
Later it will fertilize the fields.
I scrub the milkers and strainer,
up to my elbows in suds.
Dad lifts the last milk can into the cooler.
Tomorrow they'll go to the creamery.

The milk gets made into butter and cheese.
Or poured into bottles
and sold in stores and at farmers' markets
everywhere.
People in places near and far use
the milk on their cereal,
the cheese on their sandwiches,
the butter on their sweet corn.

Every morning, every night,
it's milking time.

We fan out bales of straw—
bedding for the morning—
when it will be milking time
again.
Dad opens the cooler
and takes out the pitcher of milk.
By now a thick skin of cream
floats on top.

Mom will skim it off
for morning coffee.
And I'll drink the milk,
our milk,
with my pancakes.

As the summer sun disappears
and the sky turns a dark shade of blue,
Dad and I walk up
to the house.
Single file,
on a path
worn in
the grass.

For one more night
milking time is done.
Every morning, every night,
it's milking time.

Every day of the week,
every week of the month,
every month of the year,
it's milking time.